Dear friends,

This book is a labor of my mind, heart and soul.
Born out of stillness, my inner voice insisted
on its production.

I share this love gift with everyone. If you
would like to order more copies of this book
please contact me.

And if the words touched you and enriched
your own reflections, please support my work
by passing the book forward and sharing it
with someone else

Peace and love to you,
Nita Ng
www.RunWaters.blogspot.com

Chinese Pronunciation – Pin Yin

The Pin Yin is the Romanized pronunciation for Chinese characters.

In Chinese, each character is much more than just a word. It is a symbol for a personality, for a form.

There are 4 sounds in Chinese Mandarin pronunciation. The first is represented by a (–) above the vowel in the pin yin. This mean the character is to be pronounced in a flat note.

The 2nd sound is represented by a (/) above the vowel in the pin yin. The character with this symbol above its pin yin requires a lower note than the first.

The 3rd sound is represented by a (v) above the vowel in the pin yin. This symbol represents the lowest note.

The 4th sound is represented by a (\ ) above the vowel in the pin yin. This means that the character is to be read with a high note.

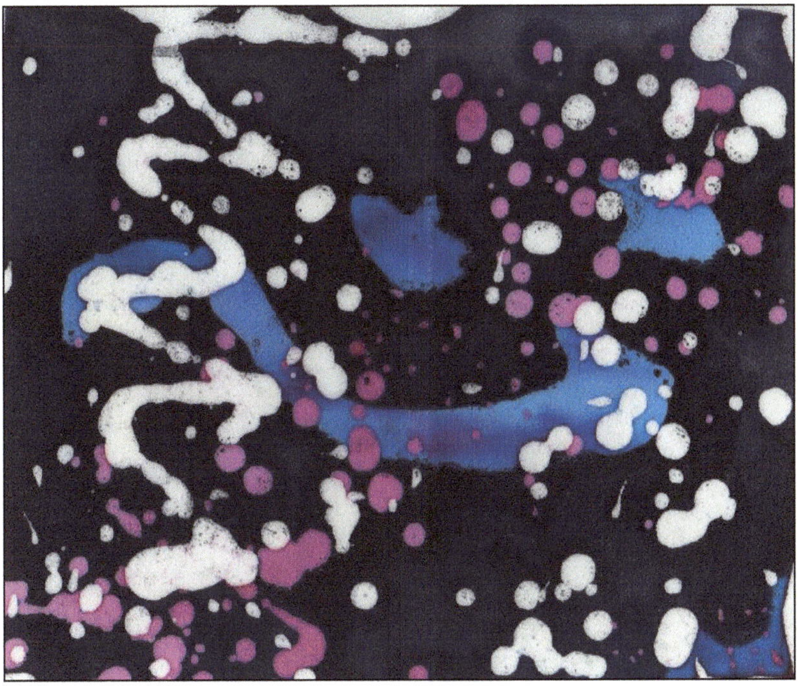

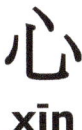

xīn

In Chinese, the character 心 is both
heart and *mind* ~ a source of
thoughts, intelligence and feelings.

All other characters in this book are
based this character, 心.

The characters in this book are organized in ascending order, according to number of brush-strokes required to write each character.

As you read this book, please pause at each page to reflect or meditate on both the paintings and the words.

Engage both the heart and the mind.
Be still.
And listen to your own heart song.

The dictionary definition of each Chinese character is the word(s) in Italics. But the whole sentence enriches the translation.

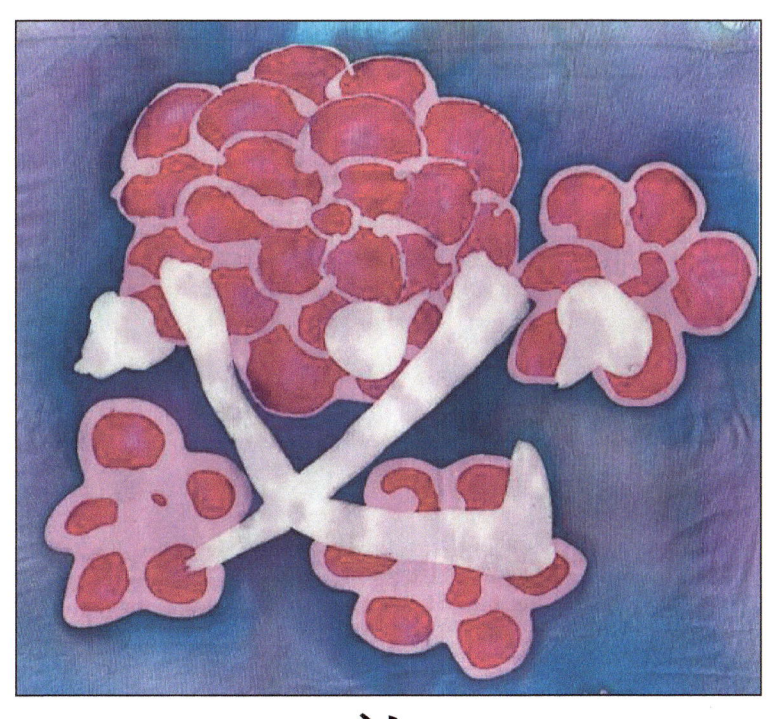

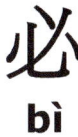
bì

Determination ~ a slash across the
heart.

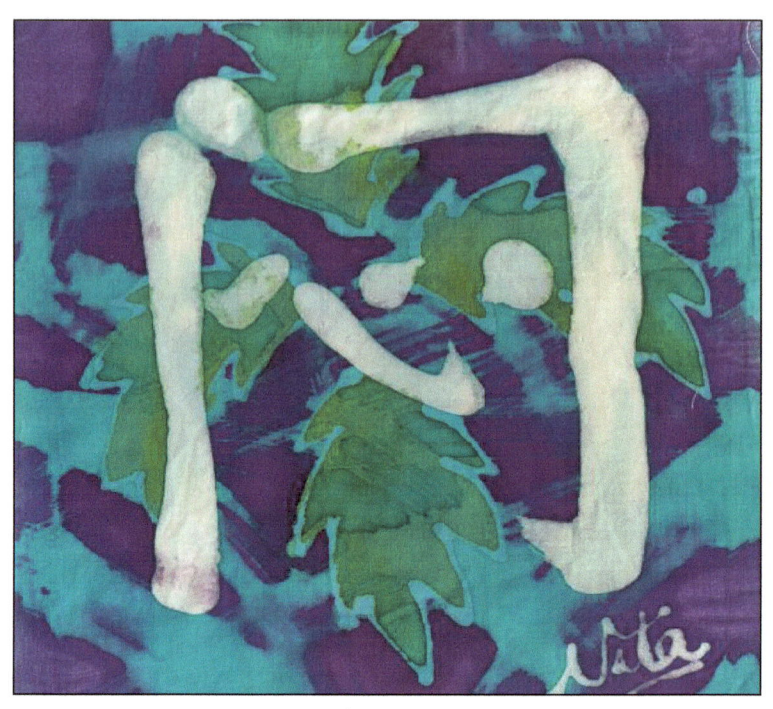

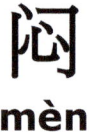

mèn

A heart that is locked behind closed
doors is a stuffy and *boring* one.

门 **mén**   *Door / house*

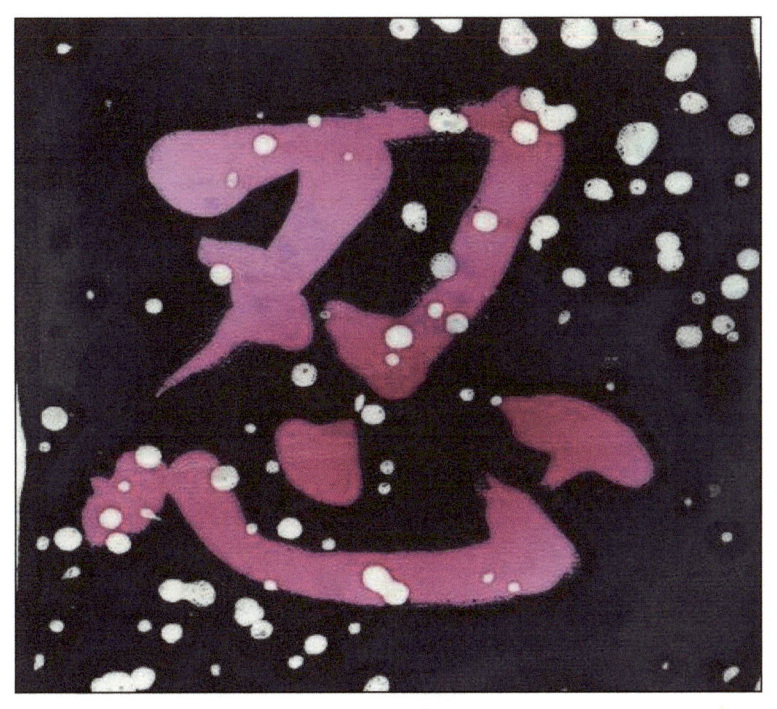

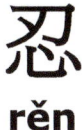

rěn

Forbearance is like stabbing a knife
into one's own heart.

刀 **dāo**   Knife

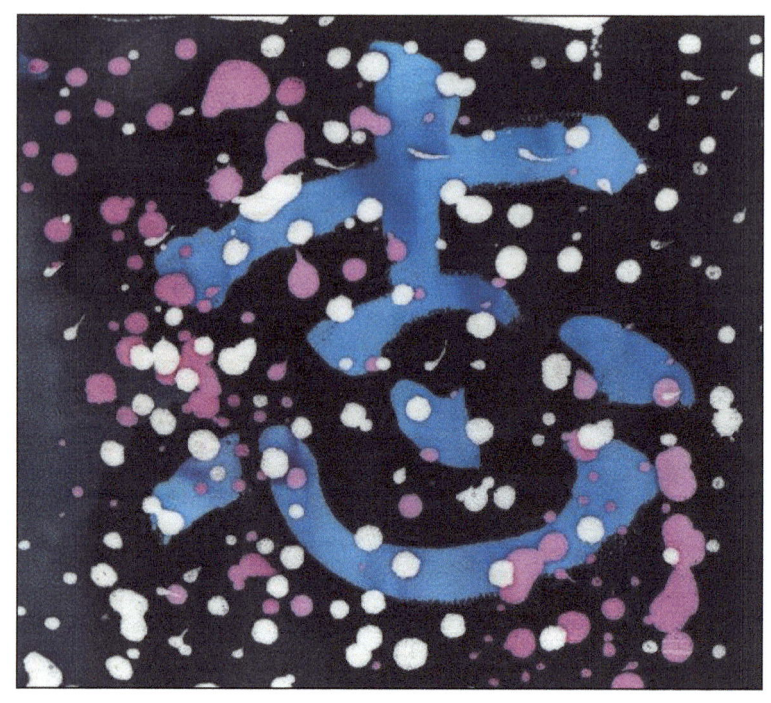

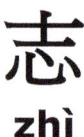
zhì

Ambition is a combination of
intelligence, skills and lots of heart.

士 **shì**   *Scholar / warrior / knight*

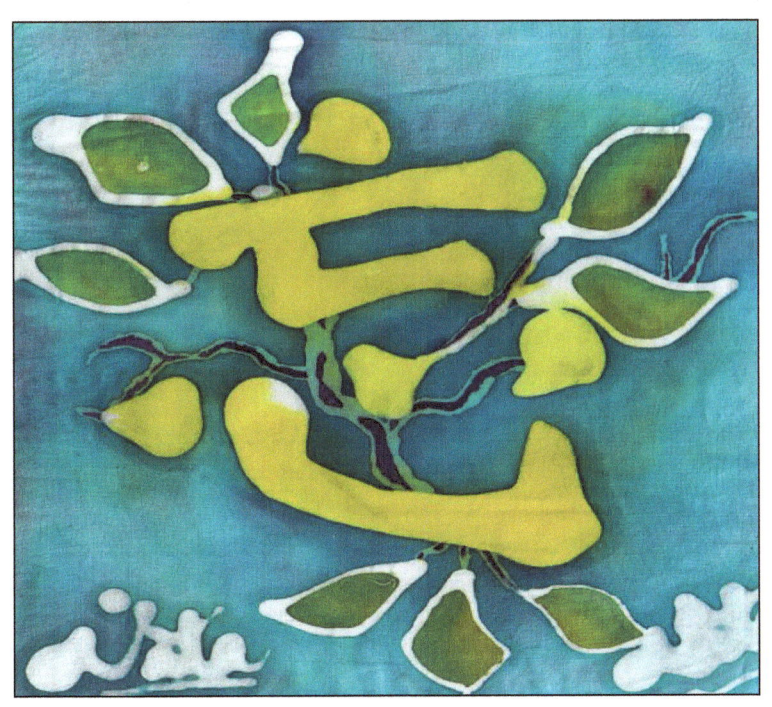

忘
wàng

To *forget* ~ the dying of one's heart.

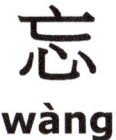 **wáng**   To die/ death

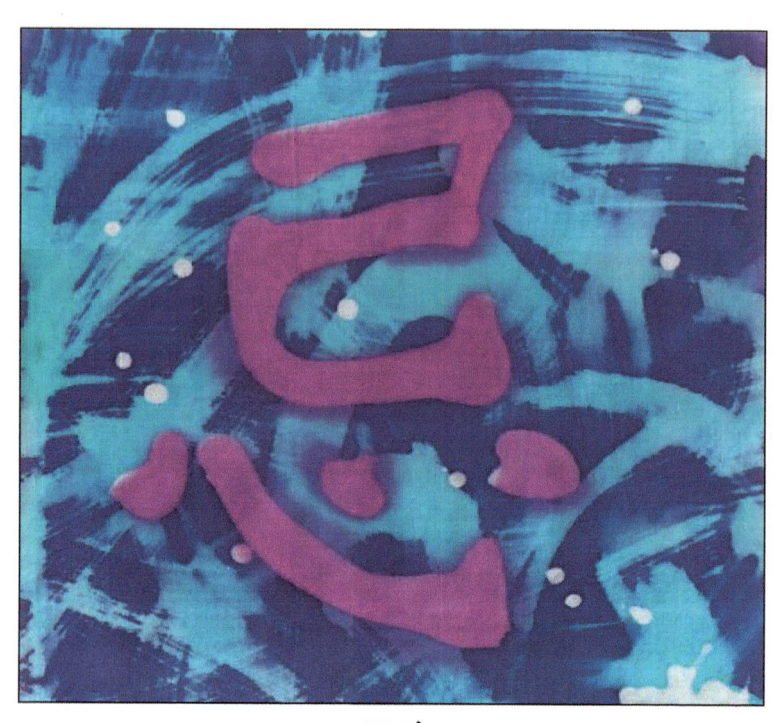

忌
jì

A jealous heart is a selfish heart.

己 **jǐ**   Self

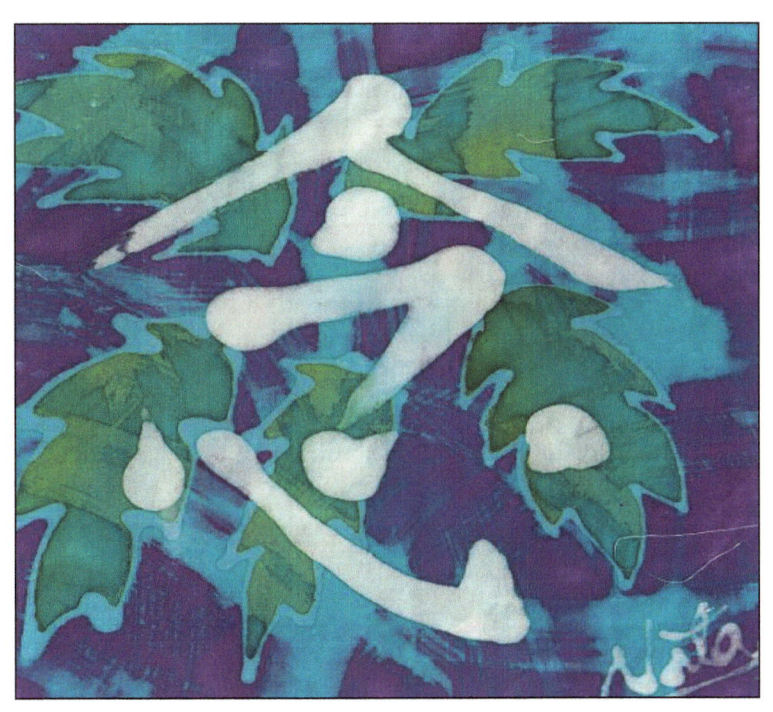

念
niàn

To remember someone is to keep him
or her present in your heart.

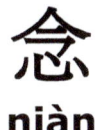 **jīn**   Today / present / current

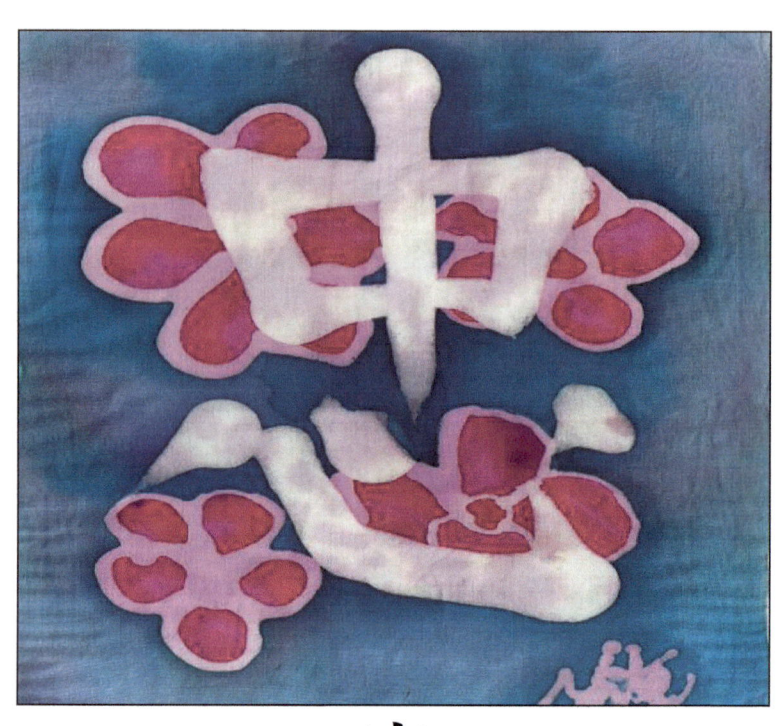

忠
zhōng

A loyal heart is a centered heart that cannot be swayed.

中 **zhōng**   *Middle / center*

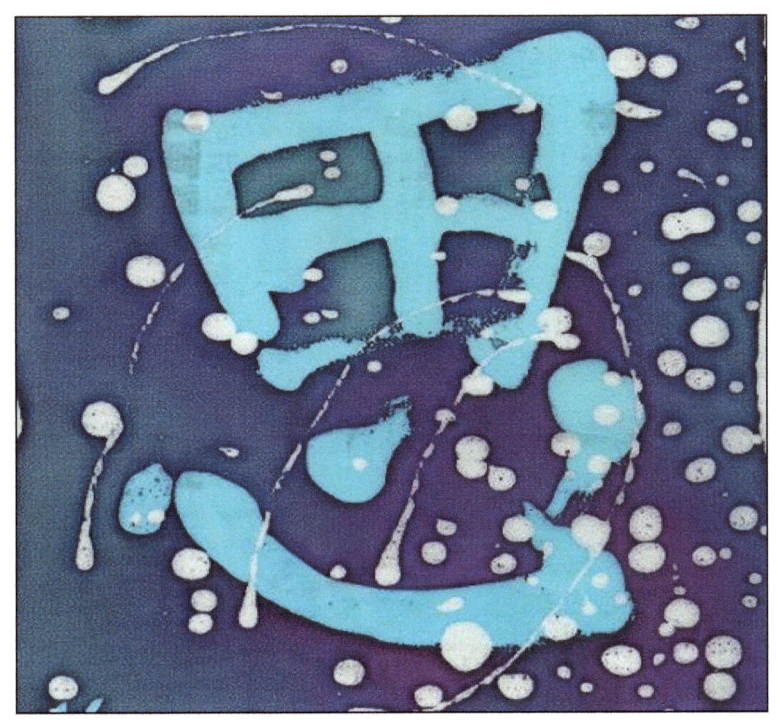

思
sī

To *consider* something is to weigh
with the heart, mind and present
circumstances.

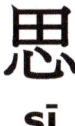 **tián**   Field / farm (livelihood)

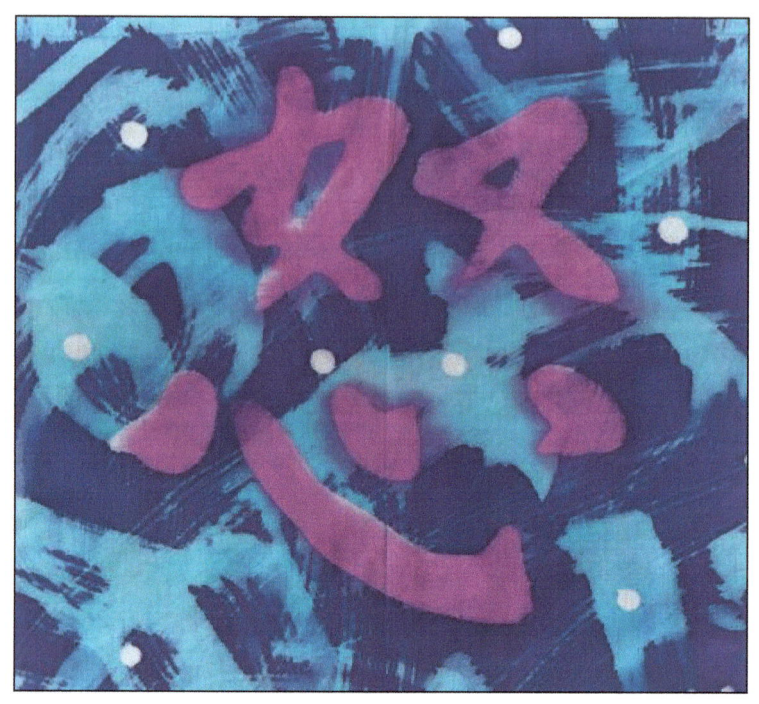

怒
nù

Fury is a passion that enslaves the heart.

奴 **nú**   Slave

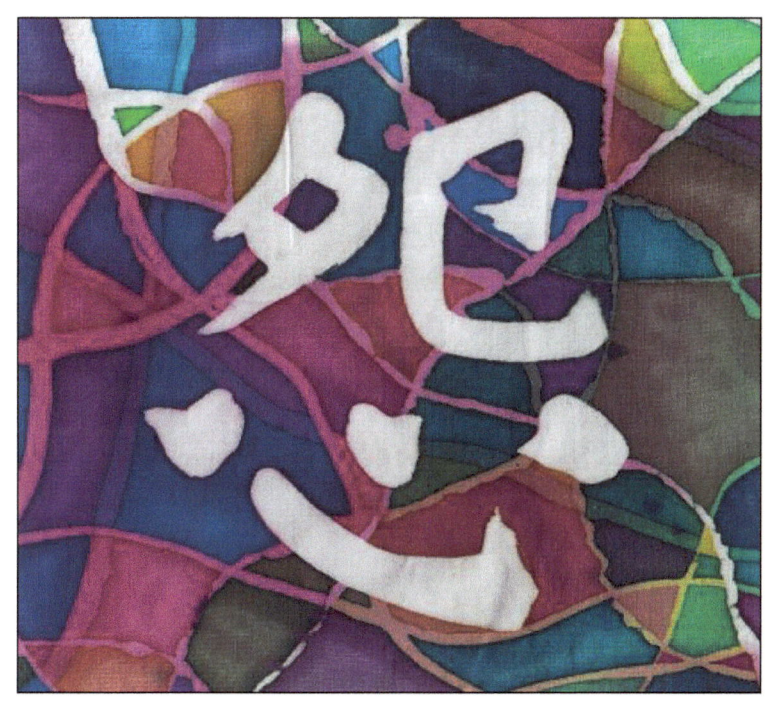

怨
yuàn

A heart that is turned away breeds
resentment.

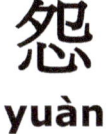 **yuàn**　　　To turn over when asleep

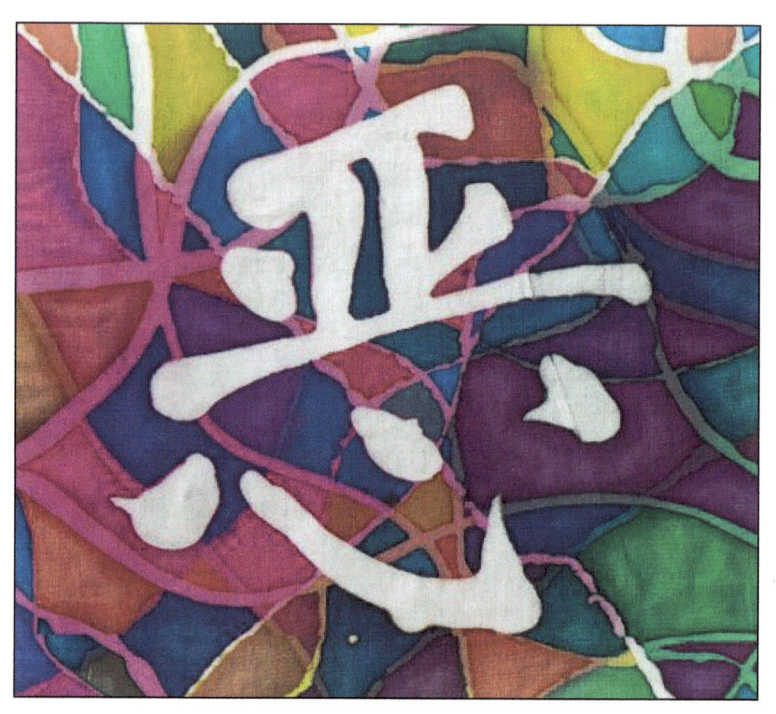

恶
è

A defective (inferior) soul is an *evil* heart.

亚 **yà**　　Inferior/ sub-standard

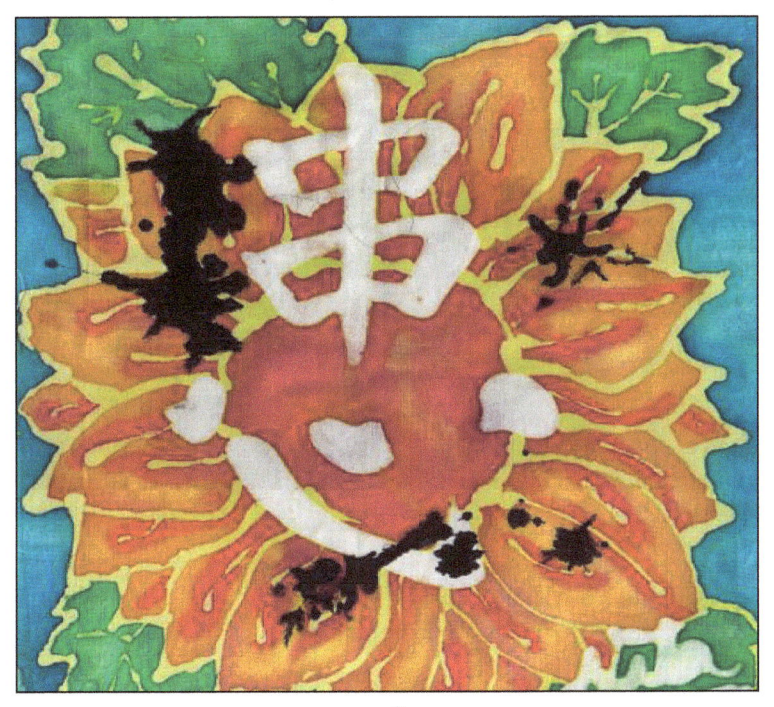

患
huàn

Strings of trouble can only bring
forth *worry* and *suffering*.

串 **chuàn**   To string together

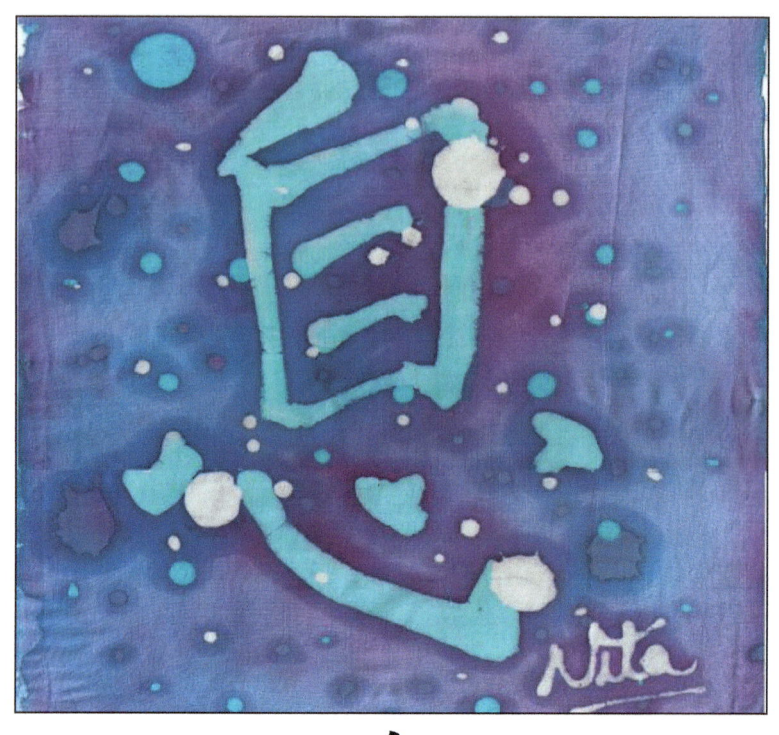

息
xī

Our *breath* is our life-force.

To *rest* is to love oneself.

自 **zì**   Oneself

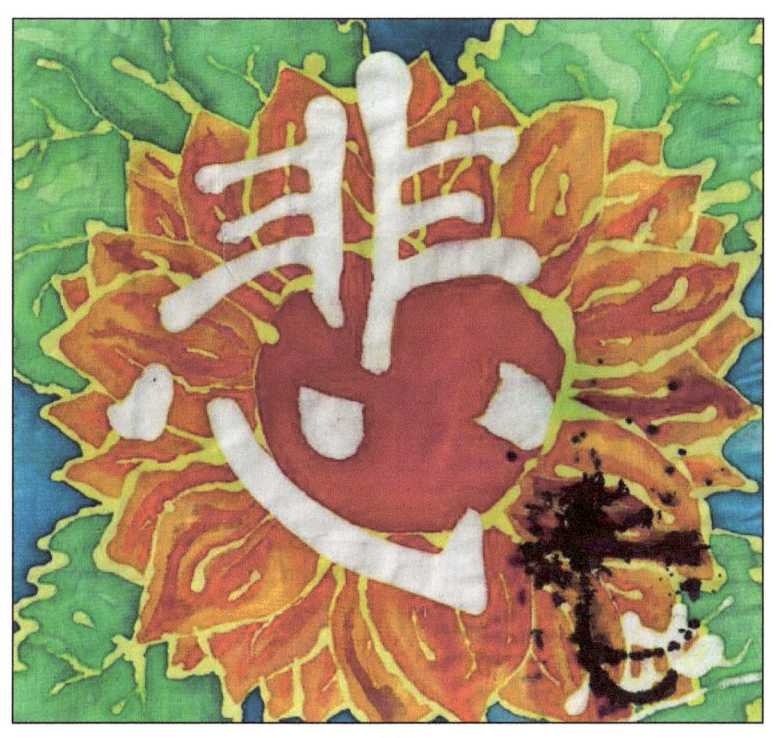

悲
bēi

Sorrow and *melancholy* should be alien to the heart.

非 **fēi**　　　Non- / not of / wrong

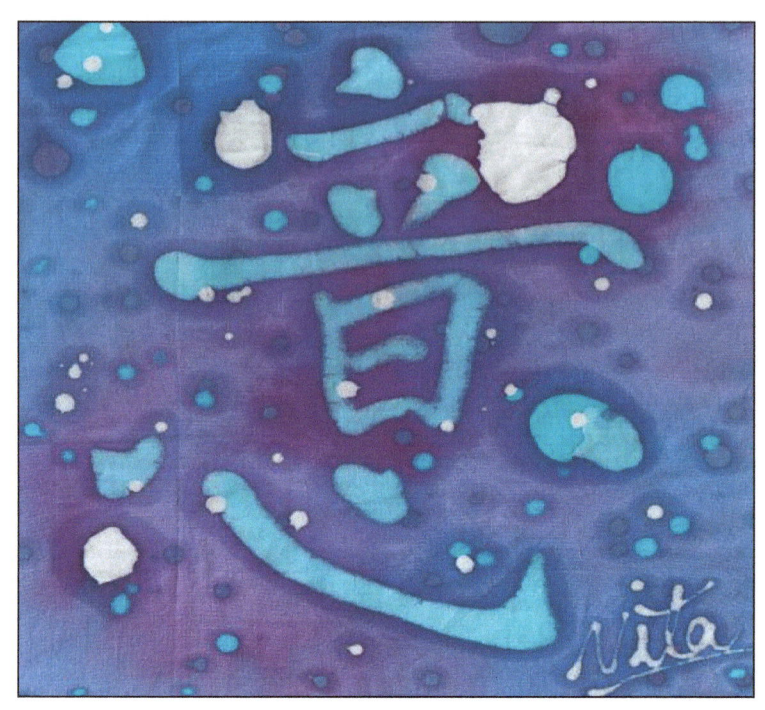

意
yì

An *idea* is a voice from the heart.

音 **yīn**   *Sound*

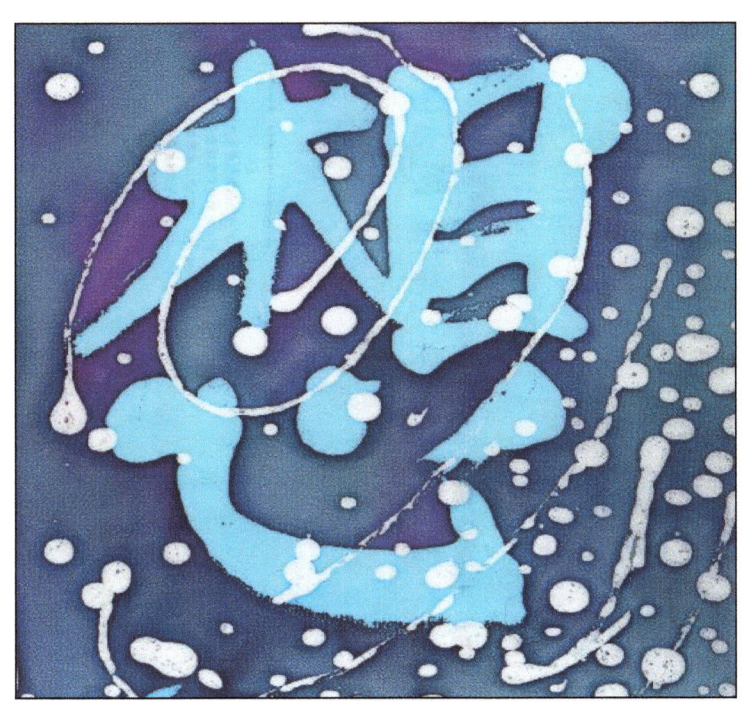

想
xiǎng

To think is a mutual meeting of
heart and mind.

相 **xiāng**   Mutually

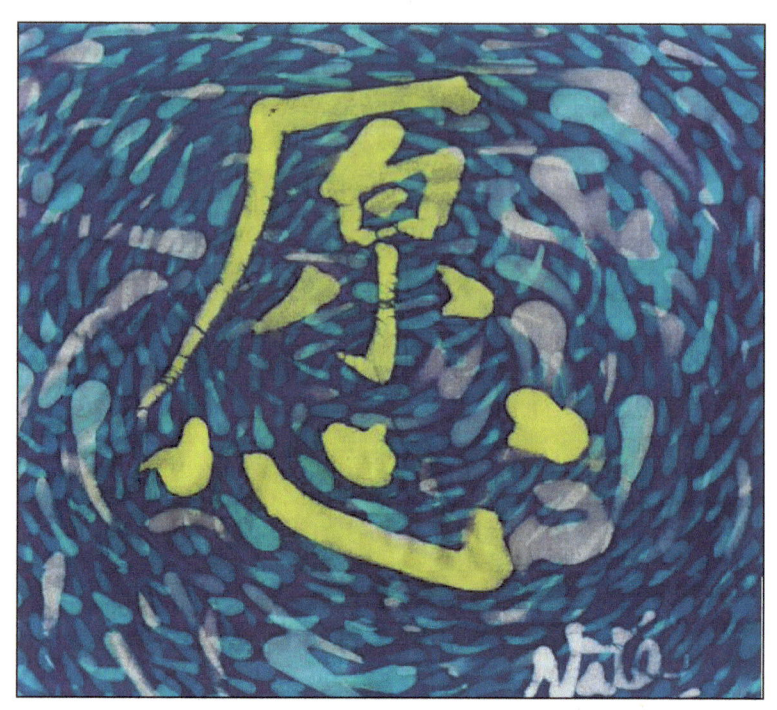

愿
yuàn

A dream is a wish that was born in the heart.

原 **yuán**　　　*Origin / cause / source*

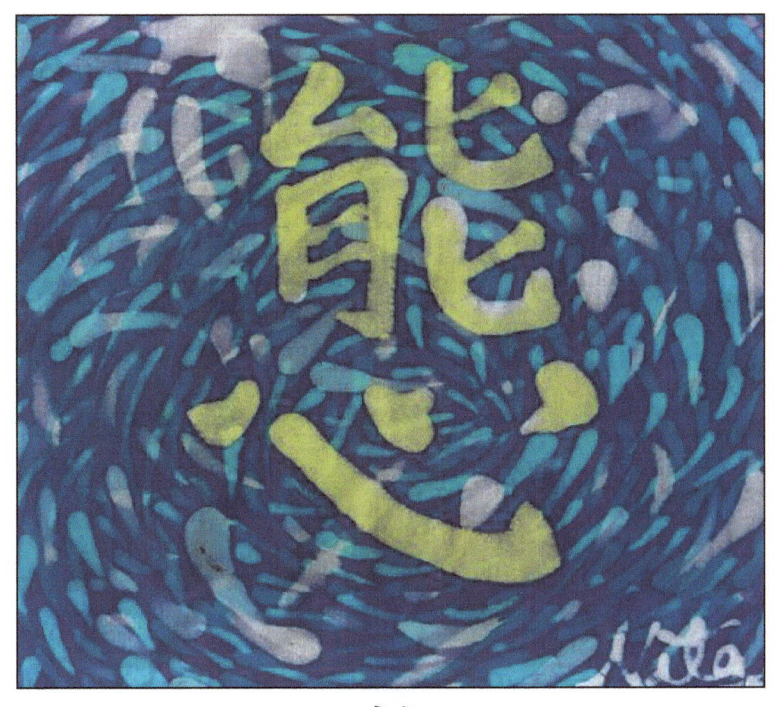

態
tài

Our attitude reflects our heart's ability.

能 **néng**   Able / capable / energy

Note: In simplified Chinese, 態 is written as 态.